Original title:
Solving the Riddle of Life (While Eating Cake)

Copyright © 2025 Creative Arts Management OÜ
All rights reserved.

Author: Maxwell Donovan
ISBN HARDBACK: 978-1-80566-165-8
ISBN PAPERBACK: 978-1-80566-460-4

Cake Crumbs of Clarity

In layers thick, the truth we seek,
With fork in hand, we giggle and peek.
Each crumb a clue, a bite full of jest,
As icing drips, we puzzle the rest.

What's life but frosting, so rich and profound?
We munch on the moments, smiles abound.
The cake is quite lofty, yet we are near,
With each joyful bite, we nibble on cheer.

A Sweet Resolution

A slice of cake to ponder and munch,
With sprinkles of laughter, we all laugh a bunch.
Each forkful carries a question or two,
But frosting's so tasty, it muddles the view.

We debate with whipped cream on all sorts of things,
While contemplating life with our sugary flings.
Should we bake or eat more? The answer must wait,
As we dive into dessert on this delicious plate.

Creamy Contemplations

What is the secret to happiness found?
In layers of chocolate, we look all around.
A dollop of cream and a dash of delight,
We nibble through chaos, all day and all night.

So maybe it's laughter that holds the key tight,
Or icing-covered giggles that make life feel right.
With cake as our guide, we dance through the mess,
In crumbs of conviction, we laugh at the guess.

Savory Puzzles

A slice of confusion, a bite of delight,
We chew on our worries, feeling so light.
Is frosting the answer? Or sprinkles some grace?
Each moment a puzzle, with smiles on our face.

The cherry on top, a whimsical sign,
With every sweet morsel, our laughter combines.
So let's feast together, share secrets and cakes,
In quests of confusion, it's joy that it makes.

A Recipe for Understanding

Mix laughter with a pinch of doubt,
Add a dollop of joy, don't leave it out.
Stir in some crumbs of curious thought,
    Bake it until the lesson is caught.

Slice it thick, share it around,
Each bite brings a truth to be found.
Sprinkle some wisdom, let it rise,
Life served sweet is the best surprise.

The Icing on the Paradox

Frosted layers hide the mess,
Each taste reveals a thoughtful guess.
Whipped cream dreams on a plate of fate,
With every bite, we contemplate.

Cherry on top, a smiley face,
In crumbs of chaos, we find our grace.
Hold your fork like a key to the fun,
Eating dessert while we ponder the run.

Eating Through the Puzzle

A slice of mystery, a fork of cheer,
Each mouthful whispers, 'Why are we here?'
Chocolate chips of insight fall,
With every bite, we question it all.

Gather the pieces, the flavors collide,
The crumbs of confusion, best served with pride.
Laughter and frosting, a curious blend,
Digesting the thoughts that never quite end.

Sugary Solutions

In the oven, ideas bake and swirl,
Pies of wisdom begin to unfurl.
Sprinkle with giggles, layer with cream,
Tasting the truth is the ultimate dream.

With each forkful, the answers stay vague,
But who cares when you've got chocolate cake?
Life's little mysteries, sweet and absurd,
Together we munch on the thoughts we've stirred.

A Pastry's Perspective

In a world of frosting bright,
I question with each bite.
Is sprinkles just for show?
Or do they help me grow?

A cherry on the top,
Should I savor, or just stop?
Is it sweet or sour fate,
Today I'll contemplate.

The Truth in Tiers

Three tiers of cake so grand,
What secrets do they demand?
With layers stacked so high,
Can laughter make me fly?

I slice into my dreams,
With frosting more than seems.
Each tier a little clue,
What am I to pursue?

Luscious Layers of Life

In luscious layers I find,
A taste that's intertwined.
Is chocolate just divine,
Or is it a grand design?

With a fork I do explore,
Every scoop unlocks more.
Between the cream and pie,
I ponder, oh so spry.

Whipped Dreams and Dilemmas

Whipped cream clouds my thoughts,
As icing fills my plots.
What's hidden in the bake?
A chance we get to take?

With each morsel I face,
Is it chaos or grace?
Just laughter shared in time,
Life's sweet and oddly prime.

The Generosity of Gelato

A scoop of joy, so cold and sweet,
Sprinkled with laughter, a tasty treat.
Beneath the sun, flavors collide,
Each bite a giggle, let joy abide.

Chasing cones on a summer's day,
As sprinkles jump and dance away.
Life's a swirl, with each new taste,
No crumb to waste, just gelato grace.

Whipped cream clouds float in delight,
With every lick, we take to flight.
In a world that's full of fun and cheers,
One scoop at a time, we shed our fears.

So here's to sweet, creamy treasures,
Finding fun in our simple pleasures.
Share your scoop and make it last,
With each cone, forget the past.

Mirthful Meringue Mysteries

Fluffy peaks on a plate so round,
With laughter baked in, joy is found.
Whisking dreams, a fanciful quest,
Pies spun together, they're simply the best.

Who knew a pastry could hold such cheer?
With every slice, a chuckle near.
Meringue clouds that tickle the nose,
Each spoonful bubbles, as giggles flow.

Life's a mix of sweet and tart,
Folded layers that warm the heart.
What's life's secret? It's filled with cream,
And a dash of fun, just like a dream.

So let's bake tales, with friends side by side,
In our meringue world, let giggles glide.
With every dessert, let's raise a cheer,
Life's full of mysteries, but cake brings near.

Flavors of Fate

Chocolate or vanilla, which to choose?
Each bite a gamble, a path we cannot refuse.
Sprinkles of destiny dance on the plate,
  Life is a party, let's celebrate fate.

Whipped cream arguments, they swirl and twirl,
While frosting friendships, we laugh and unfurl.
Taste tests of sorrow, and joys that are sweet,
  A slice of decision, with icing to greet.

Sweet Layers of Wisdom

In layers of sponge, wisdom hides deep,
Like secrets in frosting, they quietly creep.
Biting through choices, both silly and wise,
Each mouthful discovers a new kind of prize.

Marzipan lessons, fondant-filled dreams,
Riddles in pastries, bursting at seams.
Cake brings together the curious hearts,
With laughter and crumbs, let's play our parts.

Icing on My Queries

What's fluffy with frosting and melts on the tongue?
Each question's a flavor, both old and unsung.
With layers of laughter, I ponder and taste,
As chocolatey mysteries, we never waste.

Icing my worries, they suddenly lift,
Each bite a new thought, a comforting gift.
Cake conundrums, sweet battles we face,
With crumbs in our laughter, we find our grace.

Sifted Secrets

Sifted like flour, our secrets arise,
In bowls of confusion, we measure the size.
A dash of humor, a spoonful of cheer,
Mixing up answers, we savor the year.

Stirring up riddles, in batter we blend,
With giggles and sprinkles, there's no need to mend.
Life's a dessert, and we dig in deep,
Finding sweet solace in layers we keep.

The Bakery of Being

In the oven of time, we rise and swell,
Like batter that knows a delicious spell.
Whisking our worries with sugar and cream,
Life's recipe stirs, it's sweeter than dream.

Sprinkles of laughter, a dash of surprise,
Bake under the sun where the fun never lies.
Frosted with joy, we laugh at the mess,
In this clumsy kitchen, life's a grand fest!

Tasting Truths

One slice of wisdom, a nibble of doubt,
Chasing the flavors, we giggle and shout.
The crumbs of our questions scatter around,
Each bite we take, a new answer found.

Chocolate or vanilla, which one should I choose?
A fork full of laughter, how can we lose?
Whipped cream on top masks the thought of the strife,
In every sweet layer, there's a taste of life.

Pastries of the Mind

Croissants of caution, they're flaky and light,
While donuts of dreams keep our spirits bright.
Pies filled with ponderings, baked to perfection,
Each bite we savor's a thought in reflection.

Cream puffs of chaos, oh what a delight!
With layers of humor, life's troubles take flight.
Through the pastry shop of our spinning heads,
We roll with the punches, and laugh instead!

Decadent Dilemmas

A layer of choices, thick icing of fun,
With cherries on top, we race like the sun.
Should we edge on the sweet, or dabble in salt?
Each bite brings a giggle, as flavors exalt.

A cookie of chaos, a muffin of bliss,
In frosting we find that we live for the twist.
Life's tartness is fruity, a taste to explore,
With every dessert, we crave just one more!

Icing on the Mystery

In the kitchen, mess we create,
Sprinkles flying, oh what fate!
Mixing flour, a pinch of whim,
A slice of joy, or is that grim?

Juggling eggs, twirling the spoon,
Life's a dance, under the moon.
Frosting dreams, a luscious spread,
Each bite whispers, 'What lies ahead?'

Cakewalk Through Uncertainty

One foot in icing, the other in doubt,
Life's a party, so let's shout!
Baking theories with chocolate chips,
Crumby ideas on our sweet trips.

Slice of laughter, bite of surprise,
Filling our hearts with frosting pies.
Falling into layers, oh what a ride,
With every nibble, we take in stride.

Sugar-Coated Secrets

Underneath the pastel glaze,
Lie the secrets of our crazy days.
Candied puzzles, hard to break,
What's the lesson in this piece of cake?

Sprinkling joy on the plate we share,
Giggling softly without a care.
Each crumb leads to another clue,
In this dessert where dreams come true.

Bites of Enlightenment

A forkful of wisdom, oh what a thrill,
With every bite, we sip down a quill.
Life's cookbook is full of surprise,
As we nibble on truths with frosted eyes.

Chewing on choices, moist and sweet,
Every layer holds a quirky feat.
Spry with laughter, we munch and chew,
Finding clarity in gooey stew.

Tiers of Thought

In layers stacked, we ponder deep,
With frosting dreams that never sleep.
The crumbs of wisdom scattered wide,
While sugar rush ignites our stride.

Each bite reveals a comical truth,
As giggles blend with memories of youth.
We slice through doubts, with forks held high,
And laugh as questions pass us by.

A Piece of Perception

A slice of life on my dessert plate,
Chocolate thoughts that mesmerize fate.
With each sweet morsel, we take a chance,
In frosting fields, we twirl and dance.

Sprinkles of joy fall from the sky,
As icing dreams make worries fly.
What's bitter now might sweeten with time,
In every bite, a twist, a rhyme.

Sweet Moments of Revelation

With whipped cream clouds and cherry tops,
The answers come, then tumble, drop.
In every frosting swirl, we see,
The mysteries of life, a jubilee.

Beneath the layers, tales unfold,
In giggles wrapped like sugar bold.
With forks in hand, we share and tease,
The secrets whispered on the breeze.

Candied Quandaries

Wrapped in ribbon, questions await,
Is it cake or fate on my plate?
I ponder flavors, both sweet and sour,
As laughter blooms like a sugar flower.

Chewing through doubts, savoring thrills,
Each bite gives pause, as time distills.
In crumbs I find the puzzles clear,
With every forkful, I croon and cheer.

Cream-Crowned Dilemmas

In a bakery bright, I ponder and chew,
What's the answer today? Is it vanilla or blue?
With frosting so sweet, my worries dissolve,
Is life just a slice that we all must solve?

Each sprinkles a jest, each cherry a tease,
I laugh at the chaos, it's all just a breeze.
With crumbs on my hands, I think and I grin,
Who knew cake could lead to such wisdom within?

The Flavor of Insight

Chocolate layer cake whispers to me,
Do you ponder the world as you nibble on glee?
Each bite holds a truth that I can't seem to find,
Is it frosting or life that has dulled my mind?

The lemon so zesty, it tickles my thought,
Life's a pie chart of wishes, both happy and fraught.
What frosting flavors love? Is it raspberry swirl?
Or is it the fudge that makes my head whirl?

Pastry Paradox

A cupcake conundrum, adorned with a flag,
Life's choices are muffins—a sweet little snag.
Do I dive into fruit or stay in the cream?
Each bite is a mystery wrapped up in a dream.

With layers of laughter, I chew on my fate,
As sprinkles of joy help me rummage and grate.
Is it whipped cream delight or a pop of the tart?
Needing cake to decipher the riddle of heart?

The Slice of Understanding

A fork in the road or a fork on my plate?
I question my thoughts while I savor my fate.
With icing so rich and the choices so vast,
Is it cake that brings wisdom, or am I just fast?

As layers unravel with each gentle bite,
The layers of life start to look pretty bright.
With each slice I take, oh the secrets I learn,
Is the world just a bake-off? I've much more to yearn!

Tasting the Unknown

A slice of joy, a bite of fate,
With frosting thick, we contemplate.
What secrets lie beneath the cream?
Life's puzzles wrapped in a sweet dream.

The cherry on top, a flash of surprise,
With crumbs of wisdom, we optimize.
Each forkful whispers, 'What comes next?'
Unriddled laughter, we're not perplexed.

A candied clue, a chocolate swirl,
In a world of flavor, watch giggles unfurl.
Sprinkles of wonder as we partake,
Each bite a lesson, no need to break.

So raise your forks to the sugary chance,
For in frosting's embrace, we waltz and dance.
Morsels of mirth with every chew,
Life's conundrums taste better with a view.

Delights of Dilemmas

Two cakes sit side by side with glee,
One whispers, 'Pick me!' so sweetly.
The other taunts, 'I'm richer, divine!'
What a conundrum, what a sweet line!

Chocolate or vanilla, oh what a strain,
With each layer, a giggle in vain.
Frosting fights with sprinkles for fame,
In this bakery game, we all are the same.

As we ponder the cake's fate tonight,
With every mouthful, the doubts take flight.
Each slice a riddle, each crumb a jest,
In the realm of pastry, we're all guests.

So here's to the sweets, and choices so tough,
We laugh at our worries—cake's just enough.
When life hands you dilemmas, take a big bite,
And savor the chaos, it feels just right.

Midnight Cake Mysteries

At midnight, the fridge calls my name,
A cake of secrets, a delightful game.
I sneak in shadows, stealthy and neat,
What truths await in this sugary treat?

A fork in hand, a plan in the dark,
Taking my chances with every spark.
Whispers of frosting, tales yet untold,
In the depths of buttercream, mysteries unfold.

With each daring bite, I ponder and muse,
Is this just dessert or wisdom in hues?
Crumbs like confessions fall on the floor,
Sweet midnight ventures never a bore.

So let the cake haunt my dreams for a while,
With riddles and giggles, I'll share a sly smile.
For in each slice, adventure awaits,
It's midnight magic that life creates.

The Elegance of Enigma

In layers of sponge, the questions arise,
Frosted with laughter, and topped with surprise.
A delicate dance on a plate so divine,
Each bite a puzzler, oh how we dine!

With tea on the side and giggles in tow,
We nibble on secrets that nobody knows.
Cake crumbs like riddles, they scatter and roll,
In the elegance of sweetness, we find our whole.

Is it the chocolate that tickles the brain?
Or sugar-dusted icing that drives us insane?
Let's ponder our choices with forks raised in glee,
For life's little puzzles, we're happy to see.

So serve us the cake, with joy interlaced,
In the enigma of flavors, we're thoroughly based.
For life may be puzzling, but with desserts so bright,
It's the whimsical journey that feels just right.

Bites of Clarity

With frosting dreams and layers thick,
I ponder on life's little trick.
I take a bite, then furrow my brow,
Decoding flavors, I take a vow.

Each crumb reveals a hidden jest,
In sweet conundrums, I feel blessed.
Whipped cream whispers wisdom so bright,
Chocolate thoughts dance in delight.

The Pastry of Perception

A slice of pie and a fork to wield,
What truths await, my destiny sealed?
Every bite is a tiny clue,
As buttercream dreams all come true.

Flaky crusts and nutty fills,
Each taste brings laughter, my heart it thrills.
Pie charts and dessert, what a delight,
These rhymes are sweeter than a frostbit night.

Morsels of Meaning

In cupcakes lined like rows of thought,
I chase the essence, both tangled and caught.
Sprinkles of joy rain from above,
Each sugar rush, a reminder of love.

Biting deeper, I chew on fate,
With every morsel, I dare to wait.
The icing speaks in odes of glee,
As I ponder life's great mystery.

Cake as a Compass

A slice of cake, my guiding star,
Navigating life, I've come so far.
Crumbs lead me on paths unknown,
With each forkful, I've brightly grown.

Carving a laugh from fluffy layers,
These treats are more than simple players.
With a caramel map across my plate,
I laugh at fate, I truly celebrate.

Layers of Existence

In a world of chocolate froth,
We dance and laugh, no need to scoff.
Each layer stacked, a mystery spun,
With every slice, a little fun.

Sprinkles fall like dreams on plates,
We ponder all our silly fates.
With every bite, we giggle still,
Life's riddles fade with frosting thrill.

Decoding Buttercream Dreams

Whisking thoughts with buttercream,
I wonder if it's all a dream.
Cherries on top, or maybe spry,
Do they hold secrets piled up high?

A fork in hand, I take a stab,
At mysteries, oh what a grab!
Each dollop drips with comic grace,
As silly truths begin to chase.

Sweet Enigmas on a Plate

A slice of pie, a riddle served,
With whipped cream swirls, all curves unnerved.
I ponder life between each bite,
Hoping frosting sparks delight.

Life's questions rise like dough so neat,
Inside this cake, both sweet and sweet.
A giggle shared with every crumb,
In frosting fun, we find the hum.

Slices of Revelation

With every slice, unveil the jest,
In layers sweet, we're truly blessed.
The orange zest, a zest for more,
Unwrap each mystery to explore.

Beyond the crumbs, the laughter rolls,
As we take turns revealing souls.
With every punchline we create,
Sweets and smiles just can't abate.

Digging into Dualities

A slice of chocolate, a bite of cream,
Oh, what a puzzling, delicious dream!
Life's full of secrets, some sweet, some sour,
Like frosting on layers, we balance the power.

Do I want lemon or a cherry delight?
The fork in my hand gives me quite a fright!
Who knew a confection could stir such debate?
With every sweet layer, I speculate fate.

Beneath the icing, the answers lay,
Yet crumbs start to scatter, leading me astray.
With sprinkles of chaos, I navigate taste,
In this sugary quest, there's no time to waste!

As I ponder each bite with a giggle and grin,
Cake isn't just dessert, it's where we begin!
So I'll snag another forkful with glee,
In this cake-fueled journey, just let it be me!

The Dessert of Discovery

In a world full of layers, both neat and absurd,
I munch on a pastry while pondering words.
Each crumb I devour reveals a new clue,
About life's great folly and what we ought to do.

I tried a cupcake and suddenly felt wise,
The frosting gleamed brightly, oh how it deceives!
Life has its quirks, like a cherry on top,
You savor each moment, then plastic things pop.

With every cake fork, a mystery unfolds,
A sprinkle of laughter, some brave tales told.
What's next on my plate? A pie or a mousse?
Each bite is a lesson, an edible ruse!

So I bake with a fervor, these thoughts to relay,
For every sweet moment, I daringly play.
The dessert of life? A whimsical spree,
On this platter of questions, I set myself free!

Whisking Through Wonders

I stirred up confusion, I whisked up some fun,
As the batter began dancing, we knew we had won!
Each glob of the mixture was like life's tightrope,
Balancing sweetness with pockets of hope.

Mixing in flour, a splash of intrigue,
What's life without sprinkles, a dash of fatigue?
I frolic in flavors, I swirl in delight,
In the kitchen of questions, I'm taking a bite!

With ovens that chatter, we laugh at the heat,
These treats are reminders, they're silly and sweet.
A hint of diversion, a dollop of cheer,
Whisking through wonders, I'm glad I am here!

So let's serve up joy on a plate of absurd,
Each slice tells a story, each crumb is a word.
As I sink in the sweetness, what wisdom I find,
In the chaos of cake, I'm delightfully blind!

Slices of Sweet Enigmas

Hiding in layers, the secrets are near,
A slice of confusion, but oh, what a cheer!
Pecan or apple? My taste buds collide,
In this sweet conundrum, I take a big stride.

A dessert-filled dilemma, who knew it could be?
With forks poised for action, just let it be me!
Each morsel is laughter, each bite brings a grin,
In this flurry of flavor, what chaos lies within?

The great cake debate, it tickles my mind,
With every sweet piece, a new thought I find.
So I gobble up questions like frosting on pie,
In the whirls of the kitchen, I simply comply!

What's life but a platter of whims and of dreams?
With icing as wisdom, we coax out the beams.
So grab me a fork, and let's dig in deep,
For each slice of this chaos holds mysteries to keep!

The Layered Labyrinth

In layers deep, I take a bite,
What's the point? It feels so right!
Each forkful holds a secret cheer,
But crumbs can lead to strife, I fear.

With sprinkles bright and frosting thick,
I ponder life's great cosmic trick.
Is this slice of bliss a clue?
Or just a cake that's overdue?

The cherry on top might just imply,
That frosting swirls hide truths awry.
With every nibble, joy distills,
Yet does it help with unpaid bills?

So here's to cake and all its charms,
The only riddle's in its arms.
I'll munch and think, while crumbs accrue,
Perhaps a nap is what I'll do!

Frosting the Unknown

Whipped cream dreams and buttered schemes,
    Frosting clouds in sugary beams.
Each question melts beneath my fork,
    A slice of pie? Just talk the talk.

I bake my thoughts with loads of fun,
    While balancing a slice, I run.
Each layer's new, yet still the same,
Who knew dessert could be a game?

A sprinkle here, a drizzle there,
Life's puzzles hide behind each pair.
With laughter rising, cakes comply,
    To twist the truth, or let it fly.

So serve it up, this tasty mess,
And eat your cake without distress.
    In every bite, the joy is clear,
Just don't forget, the ice cream's near!

A Taste of the Infinite

A slice of cake, a scoop of thought,
In frosting's depths, the truth is sought.
What fills the heart when sugar's high?
A sprightly dance or just a sigh?

Baking life is quite the quest,
With batter mixed, I grow obsessed.
Each layer holds a hidden spire,
That makes me laugh, now that's the fire!

With candles lit, I grip my fork,
Sharing crumbs like wise old dork.
Is wisdom sweet or just a ploy?
Perhaps it all just leads to joy.

So let us bake and not confuse,
The spice of life? It's not for snooze!
For in this cake, the answer's near,
Just bite again and have no fear!

Confectionery Contemplations

In sugar shrouds, I ponder deep,
With every slice, a thought to keep.
Does frosting hide what's really there?
Or simply sweeten up my care?

Chocolate rivers, jelly streams,
Life's little puzzles burst like dreams.
Is every sprout a sign for fate?
Or just a nibble, not too great?

With every crumb, I laugh and muse,
As sprinkles cover blurry views.
Life's just a cake, with layers bold,
And icing tales yet to be told!

So pass the plate, don't overthink,
Just savor love, and have a drink!
For in this world of fun and cake,
We smile and munch, make no mistake!

The Taste of Discovery

In frosting's swirl, a question lies,
A slice of cake, oh what a prize!
Each layer whispers secrets sweet,
As crumbs of truth my heart does greet.

With chocolate fudge, I ponder deep,
What dreams awake while others sleep?
The cherry on top, a clue so bright,
A giggle here, a giggle light.

Forks dance in hand, a tasty quest,
With every bite, I feel so blessed.
The berry jam spills laughter's tune,
As sugar rush lifts thoughts at noon.

So let's delight in every slice,
For life's a treat, oh, isn't it nice?
In pastry's embrace, we find our way,
With every taste, life's puzzles play.

Puzzles in Pastry

A cookie's crunch hides riddles bold,
With peanut butter tales to be told.
Each bite a puzzle, a playful jest,
As icing laughs, it knows what's best.

Donuts roll like time's own clock,
Sprinkles of joy tick-tock, tick-tock.
Flavors merge in sweet harmony,
Like clues entwined in life's symphony.

A pie in the sky, oh what a sight,
With every fork, we take flight!
The cherry bomb, alive with glee,
In this dessert game, we're all carefree.

So grab a plate, let's share a treat,
Together in silliness, we can't be beat!
With every crumb, we'll dance and twirl,
In this culinary riddle, let laughter unfurl.

A Fork in the Path

Two cakes stand tall, which way to go?
One with lemon, the other with dough.
I pause and wonder, my fork in hand,
Which dessert choice will taste so grand?

The layer of cream beckons me near,
As sprinkles glimmer, it's hard not to cheer.
With a nibble here, and a nibble there,
Life's sweet riddles float in the air.

Each bite reveals a twist or turn,
A slice of joy, from which we learn.
Marshmallow clouds and custard skies,
In this buffet, wisdom lies.

So let us feast, both silly and wise,
With every forkful, laughter flies.
In every choice, a smile we make,
At this forked path, life is no mistake.

Balancing Sweets and Sorrows

A cupcake towers, sweet and high,
Chasing worries like clouds in the sky.
With sprinkles of joy and frosting bold,
A lesson of life in flavors untold.

A brownie's edge, sharp with delight,
Yet beneath it lies some shadows of night.
With every bite, I juggle the taste,
Balancing sorrows, it's never a waste.

A scone or two in tea's warm embrace,
With laughter shared across the space.
As crumbs fly high, and hearts grow light,
In the midst of chaos, we find what's right.

So let's celebrate this curious dance,
Of sweets and sorrows, each given a chance.
Riddles of flavor, together we seek,
In every giggle, life's truly unique.

Insights Between Layers

Layers of frosting, so divine,
Questions like sprinkles, intertwined.
As I munch on this creamy delight,
Wisdom flows slowly, taking flight.

Bite by bite, I chew on the clues,
Delicious secrets in every muse.
Cake crumbs tumble, laughter erupts,
Who knew insights came with such ups?

With each forkful, I ponder and grin,
Life's puzzling riddles tucked within.
Frosted answers, so light and sweet,
Serve up a slice, life can't be beat!

So let's celebrate this silly quest,
For sugar-coated thoughts are the best.
As I dive deeper into this treat,
I find humor in layers, oh so neat!

The Sweetness of Solitude

In quiet moments, I take a bite,
All my worries fade from sight.
Alone with frosting, my best friend,
In solitude, sweet joys blend.

Each crumb I savor gives me pause,
What's life's answer? It gives me cause.
Cake's my companion, a loyal mate,
Together we navigate this fate.

Sugar highs and contemplative sighs,
With every mouthful, the laughter flies.
A fork in one hand, the world's a game,
In joyful quietude, I'm never the same.

So here's to indulgence, a tasty muse,
Finding wisdom in chocolate-infused hues.
With each slice taken, more thoughts unfurl,
The sweetness of solitude - what a whirl!

Cakes and Contemplation

Sitting with cake, I ponder and muse,
Patchwork of thoughts, sweetened with blues.
Each layer bears the weight of the day,
I nibble the edges, dreams on display.

Crumbling edges of baked-up humor,
As icing drips like a silly rumor.
The world outside may race and whirl,
But here I sit, unfurling the swirl.

With every bite, I toss out a thought,
What matters most? Cake's that I've sought.
Like frosting, life's messy but bright,
Smiles in extension - pure delight.

So here's to moments, both frosty and fun,
When life gives questions, I'll eat 'til I'm done.
Contemplating with a spatula in hand,
The answers may come, just as they planned!

Edible Answers

In the crumbs of cake, I seek the truth,
Sifting through layers, where's my proof?
Frosting pools in a glorious mess,
Is happiness just one more slice, I guess?

The cake whispers secrets, sweet and spry,
Bubbling giggles as frosting flies high.
A fork-fueled journey through goo and glee,
Find me dreaming, cake crumbs all over me.

Laughter erupts in the sugary haze,
Questions dissolve like the frosting sways.
Is life a puzzle? Oh, what a bake!
With each giggle, I savor the cake.

So bring forth the forks, let's dive right in,
In this edible maze, I wear a wide grin.
The answers are baked into layers so bright,
Sweets of the soul bring such delight!

The Confectioner's Quandary

In a bakery bright, my mind's in a twist,
With icing and sprinkles, it's hard to resist.
Is it the chocolate or maybe the cream?
Life's mysteries linger, or so it would seem.

A cupcake winks back, with a mischievous grin,
As I ponder my choices, where do I begin?
Should I share with my friends or eat it alone?
This sweet little puzzle, I'm deep in the zone.

Slicing the layers, I search for the clue,
Maybe it's frosting that's guiding me through?
A cherry on top, or a hint of despair,
With crumbs on my chin, I really don't care.

Life's a big cake, and I'm diving right in,
What's more important, the slice or the grin?
In sprinkles I trust, as I nibble and plan,
Such wisdom from desserts, oh yes, I am a fan!

Tiers of Truth

Stacked up high, the layers call,
A cake so grand, I might just fall.
Is it just me, or did that slice wink?
With every forkful, deeper I think.

The bottom tier whispers, 'Start here, my friend,'
Do I start with the fudge, or vanilla blend?
Each bite a riddle, each crumb holds a thought,
A flavor explosion, what have I sought?

Perhaps life's a buffet, with flavors so vast,
Yet here I am, stuck with a pie crust cast.
So I savor each morsel, with laughter and cheer,
But I'm still quite puzzled, pass me another beer!

As frosting drips down, trying not to be neat,
I ponder if this is a philosophical treat.
With whipped cream on top, I feel quite alive,
In a cake-fueled conundrum, I learn, I thrive!

Cake Cravings and Cosmic Queries

A slice of life, served sweet and divine,
Where questions swirl like frosting on pine.
Do you eat the edge first or go for the core?
Such choices abound, oh what's in store!

With sprinkles like stars, my thoughts take flight,
Does cake have a meaning, or is it just bright?
Each bite is a wonder, a mouthful of glee,
What's hiding within? Could it possibly be me?

I ponder the cosmos, while icing drips slow,
Wondering where all this knowledge could go.
Can food be my GPS on this tasty quest?
Or simply a pleasure? Now that's quite the test!

So here's to the crumbs that teach us to play,
In frosting and laughter, I wish to stay.
With forks raised high, let's toast to the fun,
In the grand cake of life, we've only begun!

Frosted Reflections

A mirror of cake, so shiny and sweet,
Reflecting my thoughts as I savor each treat.
I ponder my troubles, then take a big bite,
In frosting so creamy, my worries take flight.

The layers keep talking, with secrets untold,
Encased in the sponge, like treasure in gold.
Will I find enlightenment between bites of pie?
Or is it just sugar that's making me high?

I laugh with each forkful, my giggles resound,
In a world of pure cake, there's wisdom abound.
So let's eat and ponder, it's truly a blast,
In layers of sweetness, I'll find peace at last.

As crumbs slide away, insight dances in cream,
I'll cherish these moments, like a sweet little dream.
For in every dessert, a lesson is baked,
In frosted reflections, my heart has awakened!

Confectionery Contemplations

In frosting's swirl, I ponder deep,
What secrets lie in layers steep?
With each sweet bite, I laugh and muse,
Life's not a puzzle, just flavors to choose.

Chocolate rivers run through my thoughts,
Cherries on top, life's little knots.
I nibble wisdom, creamy and light,
Is that enlightenment or just a good bite?

Sprinkles of joy on a sugary night,
Bringing forth giggles, pure delight.
Each taste is a riddle wrapped in a cream,
Maybe life's simple, or so it may seem.

So grab a fork, let's not be shy,
Questions dissolve with each slice pie.
Laughing at fate, we serve it with glee,
The cake is our compass, wild and free.

Exploring Existence with Each Slice

A slice of life on a porcelain plate,
Carrot or chocolate? I'm feeling great!
Whipped cream clouds float in my mind,
Searching for answers, they're hard to find.

With every forkful, I ponder and chew,
Do cake crumbs hold truths? Can they guide us too?
Candles flicker, their wishes grow bold,
Is making memories better than gold?

A layer of laughter, a drizzle of fun,
With frosting on top, we'll outshine the sun.
Life's just a party, we're guests in disguise,
Eating our way through the questions that rise.

So let's slice the day and serve it anew,
With sprinkles of joy and a generous view.
Cake crumbs beneath, where deep thoughts abound,
In the sweet chaos, true bliss can be found.

The Sweetness of Solitude

In quiet moments, a slice alone,
I search for answers in icing and scone.
With every nibble, I giggle and sigh,
Finding life's meaning in pie in the sky.

The solitude's sweet, like honey on toast,
In the land of the cake, I'm a jubilant ghost.
Each forkful whispers, 'Don't rush, take your time,'
As moonlight dances, and stars softly chime.

I cherish the crumbs, the mess on my plate,
In solitude's arms, I can ponder my fate.
Is life's greatest riddle a layer so sweet?
Or simply the joy of a sugary treat?

So here's to the moments where laughter runs free,
In solitude, cake is delightful company.
With every dessert, my spirits ignite,
In the quiet of sweetness, everything's right.

Edible Epiphanies

Beneath the frosting, wisdom lies,
Like sprinkles of truth in a baker's surprise.
A cherry on top, what could it mean?
Is life just a party with frosting to glean?

I chew on puzzles with every bite,
Cake crumbs scatter, what a delight!
Do layers hold tales of joy and pain?
Or just chocolate chips caught in the rain?

With each delicious question I raise,
Sweets lead to thoughts in a sugar-fueled haze.
Reality's messy like frosting smeared wide,
Finding your peace down the pastry glide.

So let's bake our woes into treats of glee,
In the oven of laughter, wild and free.
Every slice served is a truth to taste,
With edible epiphanies, none go to waste.

The Savor of Solutions

With a fork in hand, I ponder deep,
Flavors swirling, secrets to keep.
Chocolate bears wisdom, sweet and bold,
Every bite a story waiting to be told.

The frosting swirls like thoughts in my head,
Each layer whispers what hasn't been said.
Crumbs of insight dance on my plate,
As sprinkles of joy elevate my fate.

I laugh at the questions I can't seem to find,
Maybe sweetness is just a state of mind.
Digging deeper, I take a big bite,
Is it cake or a puzzle? Maybe both tonight!

Giggling softly, I chew with delight,
Feeding my brain as the answers take flight.
With each slice, a giggle escapes,
In this bakery, wisdom reshapes.

Frosty Ponderings

The frosting glistens, a mirror to browse,
What's the meaning of life? I pause and browse.
Is it in layers, sweet and divine?
Or possibly hidden in that last slice of lime?

Cupcakes call out with a playful cheer,
Telling me secrets I long to hear.
With each sugary bite, my worries dissolve,
Could cake be the key? It's time to resolve!

Giggles erupt with each sugary taste,
Thoughts drift like flour, oh! What a waste.
But laughter and frosting crumb my concern,
For wisdom's a cake that takes time to learn.

So I savor each moment, with icing and glee,
In a world full of puzzles, cake sets me free.
A slice of delight, oh what a find,
As I munch through the riddles my heart can't unwind.

Marzipan Musings

I marzipan my mind with thoughts sweet and slick,
Crafting questions like a sugared trick.
Is joy in the journey or in the cake slice?
Or is it dessert that simply suffices?

Fruits and nuts, all layered with cheer,
Each bite inspires the answers I steer.
Wisdom drizzled like caramel threads,
With a side of giggles, my hunger is fed.

Between the bites, ponder I must,
Life's flavor palette is a dessert-filled trust.
Is the secret of living a frosted delight?
Or just an illusion served up each night?

Each nibble, a mystery, sweetly perplexed,
Shall I have another, or am I vexed?
With laughter and crumbs, I leap over strife,
For marzipan musings are the spice of life!

Cakes and Conundrums

In a kitchen of chaos, my cake rises tall,
But the questions I face seem to baffle us all.
How do we slice through the layers of fate?
With sprinkles of logic that seldom await?

I fork into frosting, a puzzling affair,
Each flavor revealing a question laid bare.
Is life a sweet treat, or a bitter surprise?
My taste buds debate, while the cake quickly flies.

A layer of joy and a sprinkle of doubt,
With cakes and conundrums, I chuckle about.
The frosting holds wisdom like secrets untold,
As laughter and cake replace answers of old.

So I dive into batter and giggle with glee,
With every rich bite, life's riddles set free.
Sweetness enfolds me as humor unfolds,
As cakes hold the key to the mysteries they hold.

Flourishing Mysteries

In the kitchen, secrets swirl,
Whisking thoughts in a dreamy twirl.
Do cherries count as a life guide?
Or just sweet treats meant to hide?

Sifting flour, dreams take flight,
Life's a pastry, warm and bright.
Sprinkles scatter, choices made,
Each bite's a clue in the masquerade.

A Slice of Existence

A forkful of joy on my plate,
What does it mean to contemplate?
Carrot cake's wisdom, oh so grand,
Is it really veggies, or just a brand?

Chocolate layers, deep and wide,
Happiness melts with each sweet ride.
Frosting smiles, a sugary spree,
Life's a dessert, come taste with me.

The Sugar Truth

I ponder frosting and our fate,
Is it cream cheese or just on a plate?
Baking joy with a hint of doubt,
Life's just cake, what's it all about?

Whipping cream with a zest of cheer,
Crumbs of laughter fill the air here.
Eating slices, sharing the fun,
Every morsel, a puzzle won.

Layer Cake Logic

One layer of joy, two of surprise,
With whipped cream clouds filling the skies.
What's the answer wrapped in this dough?
Is it wisdom or just a show?

Baking batches, mixing fate,
Is vanilla essence the key to create?
A sprinkle of laughter, a dash of glee,
In the end, it's all meant to be.

Crusty Questions

In crumbs we find wisdom, so sweet,
Forks in our hands, we simply can't beat.
With every slice, new puzzles arise,
Sprinkled with laughter, while chocolate defies.

What flavors collide and what secrets they'll tell,
Is fruitwork a myth, or a cake-making spell?
A blend of confusion, a dash of surprise,
In frosting we trust, our hopes on the rise.

Oh, ponder the layers, both thick and quite thin,
What's the point of this pastry we're in?
The pie charts of life, they wiggle and squirm,
But the taste of the cake? Every bite is a term.

Whisking the questions, while icing the thought,
Each sugary answer a treasure we've sought.
So pause for a moment, enjoy all the fun,
Life's a big birthday, so let's have a bun!

Ironies in Icing

A cupcake's a puzzle, with sprinkles like fate,
Each bite is a lesson we sometimes just hate.
But look at the frosting, thick, creamy, and bold,
Surely there's solace in sweets to behold.

Life's layers get tangled, a conundrum so wide,
Chocolate or vanilla? Let flavors decide.
The sprinkles of irony dance with delight,
In the kitchen of chaos, we bake through the night.

Ah, the icing so glossy, it hides all the truth,
Could the cherry on top be the fountain of youth?
With laughter and giggles, we serve up the plights,
All while devouring our numerous bites.

So raise up your forks, let's challenge the game,
In icing we trust, there's no hint of blame.
It's all in the mixing, the flavor, and jest,
When life hands you cake, eat up and invest!

The Essence of Enigmas

The sponge may be fluffy, yet questions arise,
What lies in the filling, beneath goofy pies?
With each forkful taken, new riddles unfold,
Sugar-coated life lessons, daring and bold.

The essence of sweetness, a curious art,
With whipped cream confessions, we play every part.
As fruit flavors clash, we laugh at the fate,
Should we take the cake or just sit and debate?

Frosted conclusions drip down to the plate,
While wobbly whisks argue what's really at stake.
In doughy distractions, a side of pure cheer,
Each layer revealing what we hold dear.

So let's dig in deep, with forks made for foes,
For life's just a banquet of pastry and prose.
In the kitchen of riddles, let joy be the spark,
As we munch through the questions and dance in the dark!

Decoding Delights

With slices of wonder and frosting galore,
Every morsel whispers, 'There's something in store.'
The cake may be heavy, yet light is the mood,
As laughter erupts between bites, how crude!

Icing on top hides the mysteries deep,
While gumdrops insist that we giggle, not weep.
The secrets we taste denote layers of fun,
Decoding delights, one slice under the sun.

Did you hear the riddle baked into that pie?
Was it strawberry bliss or raspberry lie?
In chocolate we trust, but forget not the cream,
When life gives you cake, just follow the dream.

So slice up the questions, let laughter take flight,
Each cake's a diversion, a taste of pure light.
With forks raised high, we'll share each delight,
In the grand game of life—cake makes it all right!

Confections of Conundrums

A cupcake towers, sprinkles bright,
What flavor's hidden? A sweet delight.
Chocolate or vanilla, who can tell?
With every bite, we cast our spell.

Frosting mysteries, thick and bold,
A slice of cake, a secret told.
Is it red velvet or lemon zest?
Each dessert promises to be the best.

Forks in hand, we laugh and share,
Crumbs on faces, without a care.
Piecing together the fruity clues,
Life's a puzzle, like cake, we muse.

In every morsel, stories blend,
A pie's a friend, it will not offend.
With laughter and bites, we journey through,
Life's sweet riddles, we taste anew.

Edible Epiphanies

Oh, the frosting glimmers, oh, what bliss,
Bite into the mystery — did I miss?
Cherry on top, or perhaps it's lime?
Unraveling truths, one cake at a time.

Sipping on cocoa, pondering deep,
When does the frosting begin to weep?
Cookies whisper secrets, oh so sweet,
Nibbling soft doubts with every treat.

Layer by layer, we peel apart,
Discovering flavors that tug at the heart.
Is that strawberry jam or just a phase?
With every dessert, life gives us maze.

Giggles abound with whipped cream thrills,
Between bites and chuckles, inspiration spills.
So grab a fork and dive right in,
In this cake-filled journey, we all win.

Decoding the Dessert

A slice of pie on a sunny plate,
Baked with laughter and a twist of fate.
Each layer hiding a story or two,
Guess the flavor, is it apple or stew?

Crumbs are clues, we search and explore,
Marzipan messages, oh what's in store?
Chocolate chips, like fortunes, abound,
In the frosting's swirl, answers are found.

With every dessert, a tale unfolds,
Gingerbread tales are treasures of old.
Is this spice cake a hint of surprise?
In sugar-coated wisdom, we're truly wise.

Laughter mingles with each mouthful shared,
As we unearth secrets that fate had bared.
So keep your fork, and let's explore,
Each bite a riddle, forever adored.

Whipped Whispers of Truth

Creamy delights, oh what a sight,
Whispers of flavor dance in the light.
Each scoop reveals secrets from the past,
With pancakes and syrup, our spells are cast.

Laughter erupts with frosting's delight,
Is it the doughnut that holds the insight?
Sprinkled confessions in every bite,
Sharing life's truths makes everything right.

The scone knows more than it lets on,
Crusty exterior, but oh, the dawn!
Each pastry holds wisdom, old and new,
Unlocking the laughter between me and you.

So bring on the pie, the cookies, the cake,
In this sweet venture, together we make.
With whipped whispers, we savor the night,
For life's little riddles are a pure delight.

In Search of Sugary Truths

With frosting on my face, I ponder,
Is this life's sweet prize or just a blunder?
Each bite might hold a secret deep,
Or just a sugar rush that won't let me sleep.

My fork dives deep for wisdom's slice,
But is it worth the cake's high price?
With sprinkles dancing in my dreams,
I chase the truth amid whipped cream streams.

Chocolate chips like clues await,
Tangled thoughts I can't satiate.
I laugh aloud, what a funny fate,
Finding meaning on my dessert plate!

So here I sit with cake in hand,
Searching for answers, oh so grand.
In layers thick, I try to see,
Is laughter the sweetest mystery?

Small Bites, Big Questions

One small bite brings a brainy tick,
As questions dance, oh, they are quick.
Do cupcakes hold the universe's key?
Or are they just good for company?

Each crumb falls, a puzzle piece,
In between bites, I seek my peace.
With every slice, a giggly thought,
In cake, discoveries can't be bought!

I swirl my fork like a magic wand,
With every mouthful, I'm moving beyond.
Pies whisper softly, revealing their lore,
While I munch happily, ever wanting more.

Laughter echoes through frosting fog,
Amid sweet chaos, I take a slog.
For in the mess, I peek and pry,
Is the meaning of life just dessert pie?

Conundrums and Cake Crumbs

Crumbs scatter like life's puzzle bits,
As I dive into cake, my riddle fits.
Is the cherry on top the answer clear?
Or just a topping with whipped cream cheer?

I nibble soft, a thought in flight,
With chocolate layers, I feel so light.
Is joy just frosting, bright and sweet?
Or is it found in all we eat?

With laughter mixing in every bite,
Each forkful adds to the delight.
Amidst the frosting and sweet perfume,
I ponder life from my cozy room.

So here's to the cake, quirky and fun,
An answer in icing when all is done.
In every morsel, a giggle gleams,
Life's deeper meanings between the creams!

Sweet Linings of Inquiry

In layers thick, I quest for light,
Chasing answers that sparkle bright.
Does this cheesecake hold the secrets vast,
Or is its glory just a sugary blast?

I take a bite, my brain's ablaze,
In frosting smiles, I lose my gaze.
Are cupcakes just joy in a paper wrap?
Or pathways leading to a silly map?

Sprinkles rain down like thoughts of old,
Each one's a story waiting to be told.
I lick my fork, a curious grinner,
Who knew cake could make a thinker thinner?

So here's to sweets and questions galore,
Each slice a laugh, I can't ignore.
For in these moments, laughter takes cake,
And life's big questions, we gladly partake!

Sugar-Coated Secrets

With sprinkles on top and layers so sweet,
A slice of confusion, yet hard to beat.
I ponder the frosting while frosting my face,
Is life's grand plan more than just taste?

The cherry on top gives me pause for thought,
As I munch on my cake, am I wise or just caught?
The sugar rush tells me truths yet to find,
Is it frosting or wisdom that sweetens the mind?

Whispers in Frosting

The layers are thick, like mysteries grand,
Each bite is a clue, all perfectly planned.
A fork full of laughter, with frosting to share,
What's the meaning of life? I can't help but stare.

When icing drips down like secrets untold,
I nibble on truths both bitter and bold.
Amidst giggles and crumbs, I find what I seek,
Is the secret to living just having a peek?

Crumbs of Wisdom

Crumbs on the table, crumbs on my chin,
Each morsel of cake helps unravel the din.
A cake full of fiber, a sweet slice of lore,
Could this be the answer to all I implore?

With chocolate and laughter, I giggle with glee,
A paradox formed in my slice of spree.
Each little bite whispers, 'Just take a chance,'
Do I get my cake and the wisdom to dance?

The Cake and the Conundrum

I slice into layers, each one a new dare,
The frosting conundrum floats sweet in the air.
With bites of banana and sprinkles of fate,
Is this riddle of life more dessert on my plate?

As laughter and frosting collide on my face,
I ponder if wisdom is found in the chase.
The cake gives me humor, a slice of the truth,
In sugar-coated moments, I reclaim my youth.

Crumbs of Clarity

In a world of frosting dreams,
I search for answers, it seems.
A slice of joy, a dash of doubt,
With every bite, I twist and shout.

A cherry on top, a riddle chin,
Where do I start, where do I begin?
The crumbs beneath tell stories old,
Or is it just icing that's gone cold?

With sprinkles scattered all around,
I ponder life while cake's been found.
Each flavor bursts, a silly thought,
Is this what wisdom really sought?

So here I sit, fork in hand,
Dancing with cake, oh so grand.
Laughing at puzzles, small and sweet,
Life's a treat, it's cake we eat!

Frosted Questions

What's the secret hiding in this pie?
With frosting swirls, I give a sigh.
Should I ask, or just take a bite?
In this sugary realm, all feels right.

Finding truth in each layer's fold,
Do sprinkles hold wisdom, untold?
A creamy confusion layers my brain,
But with each nibble, I feel sane.

Is it chocolate, or red velvet bliss?
Perhaps life's truth tastes like this?
I chuckle and chew, questions arise,
Is the answer hiding in dessert pies?

So I'll nibble slowly, with a grin,
Playing the fool for the fun I win.
Life's cake is messy and sweet, it seems,
Maybe the answers are just silly dreams.

Layers of Existence

Beneath the frosting's shiny dome,
Layers of life twist and roam.
Vanilla whispers, chocolate cries,
Each bite reveals sweet, strange lies.

With a fork in hand, the truth I seek,
In every crumb, a clue so sleek.
Do cherries hold the key to fate?
Or does icing seal a different state?

Sifting through layers, oh what a ride,
Can laughter be found at the cake side?
As gooey layers watch me ponder,
Is the meaning just cake to wander?

So I dive deep in frosting's art,
Mixed metaphors swirl in my heart.
Each slice I take, a laugh or two,
Life's a party, with cake for the view!

The Cake of Knowing

In a bakery of thoughts, I chase,
The creamy dreams I dare to face.
Each icing swirl a giggle or snort,
In this confectionery merry fort.

Sweet slices whisper secrets discreet,
Is knowledge just sugar, oh so sweet?
With every bite, the questions grow,
What do I really, truly know?

I lick my fingers, crumbs aglow,
While figures dance, putting on a show.
Fork in hand, I stare at the cake,
Should I ponder or just partake?

With laughter echoing in the air,
I munch on life without a care.
So let's celebrate, and take a chance,
In the world of cake, let's all dance!

www.ingramcontent.com/pod-product-compliance
Lightning Source LLC
Chambersburg PA
CBHW051651160426
43209CB00004B/870